G000320382

WALSINGHAM

England's Nazareth

Peter Rollings

WALSINGHAM

England's Nazareth

An account of England's
National Shrine

of

Our Lady at Walsingham

Peter Rollings

AD MAJOREM DEI GLORIAM

ET DEI GENETRICIS HONOREM.

Published by R. C. National Shrine, Walsingham

First published in 1998 by the R. C. National Shrine,
Pilgrim Bureau, Friday Market,
Walsingham, Norfolk, NR22 6EG.

All rights reserved.
No part of this publication which is copyright
may be reproduced, stored in a retrieval system,
or transmitted, in any form or by any means, electronic,
mechanical, photocopying, recording, or otherwise,
without the prior permission of the publishers.

Copyright © R. C. National Shrine, Walsingham, 1998

ISBN 0 9502167 3 9

Printed by
The Lanceni Press Ltd, Fakenham, Norfolk

A Walsingham Centenary Publication

1.   Walsingham 100 Years of Pilgrimage 1897 - 1997
      (R. C. National Shrine, 1997)

2.   Walsingham England's Nazareth by Peter Rollings
      (R. C. National Shrine, 1998)

Front and Back cover Slipper Chapel photographs and that on page 74
reproduced by kind permission of Fr. Peter Murray, s.m.

FOREWORD

Fr. Peter Rollings is well-known to many of our pilgrims in Walsingham and I am delighted to commend this history of England's National Shrine to a wider readership.

It is now over one hundred years ago that pilgrims began to return to Walsingham after the suppression of the ancient Shrine of Our Lady of Walsingham. Fr. Peter's book is one of a series published by the National Shrine to mark this Centenary. It is my hope that a renewed understanding of our rich heritage in Walsingham will inspire even more pilgrims to find God in England's Nazareth.

Fr. Alan Williams, s.m.
Director of the National Shrine

Solemnity of Mary, the Mother of God,
1st January 1998.

ACKNOWLEDGEMENTS

I would like to record thanks to Fr. Peter Allen, s.m. for introducing me to Walsingham, to Fr. Roland Connelly, s.m. and Claude Fisher for stimulating my interest in Walsingham's history. Also to the Shrine staff for their continued support especially to Fr. Alan Williams, s.m., Tim McDonald, Anne Milton and Debbie Parker for proof-reading; to Anne for her help in the Archives and to Debbie for preparing the manuscript for publication.

P.R.

CONTENTS

INTRODUCTION

Since 1061, Walsingham has been venerated as one of the holiest places in England. It is held that it was at Our Lady's own request that there should be a Shrine in Walsingham. It was founded at the time of the Crusades when it was impossible to visit the Holy Land and so English Catholics were able to visit Nazareth in their own land for it is from Nazareth that Walsingham takes its inspiration.

From wills and bequests from all over the country it seems that Walsingham was more than a mere local Shrine. In fact, it was held to be the duty of every Englishman that at some time during his life he should visit Our Lady at Walsingham. The Elizabethan chronicler, Holinshed, writing after the destruction of the Shrine still puts Walsingham first among the roads of England.

Nor was devotion to Walsingham restricted to England. J. C. Dickinson, in his Monastic Life in Medieval England, says "Our Lady of Walsingham was one of the few English pilgrimages to attract some following from abroad and on the eve of the Reformation was easily the most popular Shrine of its kind." It was counted as one of the four major shrines of Christendom, ranking beside Jerusalem, Rome and Compostella.

In fact, Walsingham was so popular that the Milky Way was renamed the "Walsingham Way" because its myriad stars resembled the crowds thronging to the Shrine. But the past is not all that remains of this ancient Shrine. Walsingham is not just a monument or an historical curiosity. It is a living reality with a practical relevance for today as much as for any other age.

These pages are an attempt to put together what is known of Walsingham's history and to put it into context with the living devotion and the life of the Church. Much of what follows has appeared in other forms and most of it can be found in the books listed in the Sources Consulted at the end. What the present work attempts is to provide a synthesis of these in a manageable form and the reader is referred to the works listed for a fuller treatment of the matter.

P. Rollings

PILGRIMAGES

One of the themes of the Second Vatican Council is that of the Church as a pilgrim here on earth.

> "The Church to which we are all called in Christ Jesus, and in which by the grace of God we acquire holiness will receive its perfection only in the glory of heaven, when will come the time of the renewal of all things .... However, until there be realised new heavens and a new earth in which justice dwells, the pilgrim Church, in its sacraments and institutions, which belong to this present age, carries the mark of this world which will pass, and she herself takes her place among the creatures which groan and travail yet and await the revelation of the sons of God." (Lumen Gentium 7:48).

The Church, then, journeys through the world towards her final goal which is the kingdom of God. The goal is as yet unattained and so the pilgrim is never at rest. The pilgrimage to a shrine such as Walsingham is a symbol of the Church's great journey and when the pilgrim joins the community at the shrine he becomes more conscious of his part in the community united to the Lord and the Church triumphant and of the unity which exists between Christ and his body of which we and the saints are members together. In some way by a pilgrimage we are brought deeper into the mystery of our salvation in Christ which is still to be striven for and yet already attained.

Pope Pius XII had this to say about pilgrimages in 1952:

> "The pilgrim's journey is long, and begins with a parting. He leaves his home, his everyday life, and forgets all his unimportant trivial cares and then sets off courageously and so prayer makes its way to God more easily. The company of other pilgrims increases the ardour of his soul and gives rise to prayer in

common, singing, exchange of thoughts and feelings. It culmi-
nates in restrained exultation when at the altar Christ offered in
sacrifice comes with his body to strengthen the Christian on the
way to God. The pilgrimage reawakens in you the spirit of
penance, the sense of Providence and trust in God. It instructs
you afresh about the meaning of life: to turn away from the present, from everyday joys and sorrows, and to turn towards the
goal whose radiance shines on you."

(Sacramentum Mundi vol. 5, p.27).

In the later Middle Ages, about the time when Walsingham was most
popular, there were so many people wanting to make pilgrimages to various
places that the Church had to regulate the practice so that families and work
were not neglected. A pilgrim had to have permission from his Bishop
before setting out and he had to put his affairs in order. He would often
make his Will and he had to repay any outstanding debts and provide for his
family in his absence. Then the pilgrims would assemble in their parish
church were they would be invested with the distinctive habit of the pilgrim
blessed by the priest. Pilgrims usually wore a beard and a long grey gown
with a cowl and a broad hat. They carried a scrip, bottle and staff. Mass
was celebrated and a final blessing given and then the pilgrims set out.

The routes were marked with wayside crosses, but it was not unusual for
pilgrims to get lost or even to be deliberately misled. There were also many
station chapels where the pilgrims would stop to rest and pray. Monasteries
and hospices afforded hospitality such as the one founded for poor pilgrims
about 1224 by William de Bec at Billingford near Norwich.

On their return, the pilgrims wore badges to show which pilgrimages they
had made. Perhaps the best known of these is the scallop shell of Saint
James at Compostella. The Walsingham emblems which have been found
vary in shape and design but usually bore a symbol of the Annunciation.

Pilgrims were not always held in high esteem however. Many thought that they had taken to the road in order to shirk their responsibilities and this was probably true of some cases. Langland says as much in <u>Piers Plowman</u> in 1362:

> "A host of hermits with hocked staves
> Went to Walsingham with their wenches behind them,
> These great lubbers and long, who were loath to labour,
> Clothed themselves in copes to be distinguished from others,
> And robed themselves as hermits to roam at their leisure."

Nor were the bands of pilgrims well-received wherever they went. In 1407, William Thorpe, a Lollard, complained they:

> "will ordain to have with them both men and women
> that can well sing wanton songs:
> and some other pilgrims will have with them bagpipes:
> so that in every town they come through,
> what with the noise of their singing,
> and with the sound of their piping,
> and with the jingling of their Canterbury bells,
> and with the barking out of the dogs after them,
> they make more noise than if the King came
> there away with all his clarions and other minstrels.
> And if these men and women be a month in their pilgrimage,
> many of them shall be an half year after great janglers,
> tale tellers and liars."

(Fr. Whatmore's <u>Highway to Walsingham</u> p.13)

But Thorpe was brought before Archbishop Arundel who said:

> "Thou seest not far enough in this matter, for thou con-
> siderest not the great travail of pilgrims, therefore thou
> blamest the thing which is praisable. I say to thee that it
> is right well done that pilgrims have with them both
> singers and also pipers, that when one of them that goeth
> barefoot striketh his toe upon a stone, and hurteth him
> sore, and maketh him to bleed, it is well done that he or
> his fellow then begin a song or else take out of his bosom
> a bagpipe, for to drive away with such mirth the hurt of
> his fellow. For with such solace the travel and weariness
> of pilgrims is lightly and merrily brought forth."

(Fr. Whatmore's <u>Highway to Walsingham</u> p.13)

In spirit, though not often in mode of travel, the modern pilgrimage is not essentially that different from those of old and when we look at the complexity of our way of life, perhaps the practice is all the more needed.

THE SLIPPER CHAPEL

The routes that pilgrims took to Walsingham covered all England. The main way was from London by way of Ware, Newmarket, Brandon, Necton, Hempton and East Barsham. (Fr. Whatmore's <u>Highway to Walsingham</u> follows this route). From the North, pilgrims crossed the Wash near Long Sutton and came through King's Lynn (then called Bishop's Lynn) and Flitcham, Rudham and Coxford. From the East pilgrims came by Norwich and Attlebridge. The routes were marked by stone crosses and studded with shrines and station chapels as stopping places. The Slipper Chapel, just over a mile outside Walsingham, is the last of these. It is 117 miles from London by the old pilgrim's way, 27 miles from Norwich, 26 miles from King's Lynn and five miles from Wells-next-the-Sea.

The Chapel is commonly called the Slipper Chapel. This may have been because pilgrims removed their shoes here in penance and humility before setting foot on the Holy Land of Walsingham, but the name is just as likely to come from the old English word "slype" meaning "something in between", the Chapel standing, as it does, between the rest of the world and Walsingham.

St. Catherine of Alexandria, patroness of pilgrims, is the saint to whom the Slipper Chapel is dedicated and the Chapel is so orientated to the South East that the sun rises directly behind the Altar on her Feast Day, 25th November. There is also a Chapel of St. Catherine of Alexandria one mile outside Nazareth which was protected by the Knights of St. Catherine.

St. Catherine is traditionally said to have been buried on Mount Sinai and according to Martin Gillett, apart from Nazareth itself, Mount Sinai is the oldest shrine of the Annunciation. There is evidence that as early as the year 385 there was a church there dedicated to Our Lady. The church on Mount Sinai is so orientated that when the sun rises on 25th March (old style), the Feast of the Annunciation, its rays come through an aperture in the wall beneath the altar of the Burning Bush and across the traditional site of the root of the Bush. The altar is surrounded by icons representing the tradition attested to by the early Fathers that when Moses removed his shoes and stepped forward to see the vision of God in the Burning Bush he in fact saw the image of the Blessed Mother with her Child. These things cannot have been far from the minds of our fathers when they designed and built the Slipper Chapel.

The usual date for the building of the Slipper Chapel is given as 1338 but it could have been as late as 1360 or even 1380. It is certainly mid to late 14th Century. It is said that Alan of Walsingham may have been the architect because of similarities between the Chapel and the lantern of Ely Cathedral for which Alan was responsible. It is of the late decorated period and has been described as one of the architectural gems of 14th Century England. Most of the building including the chestnut roof timbers is original. It measures just 28 feet 6 inches by 12 feet 5 inches which make it just a little larger than the Holy House which Richeldis built in Walsingham in 1061.

When the Priory and the Shrine were destroyed in 1538, the Slipper Chapel escaped unhurt. For a short time it seems it continued in use as a Chapel and then as a poorhouse, a forge, a barn and a byre. By 1863 when Miss Charlotte Boyd first saw it the Chapel was neglected and had two cottages built against its North side. In the early decades of this century the caretaker could remember seeing men threshing corn on its floor.

There are grounds, however, for believing that the Slipper Chapel was never totally neglected by Catholics. Mgr. Laurence Emery reports a conversation he had in 1938 with an old man who used to live at the Slipper Chapel in his youth. During his boyhood, his father would be frequently angered and surprised by Catholics asking permission to visit the barn where they would kneel and pray. This would be in the 1860's and the man could remember his grandfather complaining that this had gone on when he was a boy and this would take us back to at least 1800, a time when the Catholic Church in England was at its lowest ebb.

Miss Charlotte Boyd

In 1863, Miss Charlotte Boyd, who was an Anglican dedicated to restoring Benedictine monasticism to the Church of England, visited the Slipper Chapel and saw it in a ruinous condition for which neglect she upbraided Mr. Lee Warner who owned it. She also unsuccessfully tried to buy the Priory, the original site of the Shrine. Miss Boyd was dedicated to Benedictine monasticism and as the nearby church of St. Giles in Houghton le Dale belonged once to the Benedictines of Horsham St. Faith near Norwich, it seemed likely that the Slipper Chapel was also theirs and so she was determined to have it for a convent. In fact, Martin Gillett reckoned that the boundary of the Benedictine property was the River Stiffkey and so the chapel probably belonged to the Augustinians at the Priory.

On 5th January 1894, an agreement to sell the chapel for £400 was signed by Mr. Lee Warner of Walsingham Abbey. After many legal difficulties the deal was completed on 26th June 1896. Meanwhile, during a retreat in Bruges, Miss Boyd became a Catholic in September 1894 and in 1895 she became an Oblate of Downside. Charlotte offered the Chapel to the Benedictines asking that it should be used for all time as a place of prayer and penance for unity in England. The monks advised her to offer it to the Bishop of Northampton, Arthur Riddell. Bishop Riddell accepted the

Chapel on 5th August 1895 but he saw it only as a mission chapel whereas Miss Boyd was determined that it should be something more. In June 1897 she withdrew her offer and gave the Slipper Chapel to the Downside Community.

Without the permission of the Bishop, there was no chance of the Slipper Chapel becoming a Shrine or anything else and so it lay unused. The Parish Church of the area at King's Lynn became the focal point when the Shrine of Our Lady of Walsingham was re-founded in 1897. It was housed in a specially built Lady Chapel, which, unfortunately, is based on the later Shrine at Loreto and it contains a copy of the image of Our Lady of Cosmedin given by Pope Leo XIII. However, the parish priest at the time, Fr. George Wrigglesworth, shared the hope that the Shrine

Shrine at King's Lynn

would eventually be restored to Walsingham and on the day after the dedication of the King's Lynn shrine he led a pilgrimage to the Slipper Chapel. This is counted as the first pilgrimage of modern times.

In 1897, Thomas Garner, an eminent Victorian Architect, was commissioned by Charlotte Boyd to restore the Chapel. He had already been employed by her to restore the gatehouse at Malling Abbey. He was also responsible for the crucifix in the reredos of Winchester Cathedral, the altar-piece (now bombed) of St. Paul's Cathedral and for the choir of Downside Abbey. Work began in May 1897, the work on the masonry being carried out by craftsmen from the Cambridge firm of Rattee and Kett. Charlotte had outlined plans for the interior of the Chapel, but these were not fulfilled until almost thirty years after her death. (She died on 3rd April 1906 in London).

In 1930, the Benedictine Community at Downside gave the Slipper Chapel to the Diocese of Northampton. A plaque in the cloister at the Chapel commemorates this. On 15th August 1934, the Feast of the Assumption of Our Lady, Bishop Youens of Northampton celebrated the first public Mass in the Slipper Chapel for 400 years.

The new Shrine was given by Miss Hilda Cary in memory of her brother, Launcelot, who was a Lieutenant in the 9th Battalion, the Devonshire Regiment, and who was killed in action in the Great War. Mrs. Chapman gave two fine Florentine candlesticks in memory of her son, Maurice, who died in 1931. The first modern statue was designed by Professor E. W. Tristram from details on the 15th Century seal of the Priory. It was enthroned on 19th August 1934 at the first National Pilgrimage and on that occasion the Bishops of England and Wales, with the approval of the Pope, designated the Slipper Chapel as the National Shrine of Our Lady for England.

The fine reredos of the altar depicting the crucifixion and Saints Catherine of Alexandria and Lawrence the Deacon was carved in 1934 by two Walsingham artists, James and Lilian Dagless. In 1936, they carved and decorated the canopy and pedestal for the statue.

Additions were made to the Slipper Chapel in 1938. An extra Chapel providing an additional altar dedicated to the Holy Ghost and a much-needed sacristy were joined to the Slipper Chapel by a short cloister. On

Cloister and Holy Ghost Chapel under construction

8th September 1938, Our Lady's Birthday, the chapels were consecrated. In 1953, a new East window was erected to commemorate the definition of the dogma of Our Lady's Assumption. It was the last work of the artist, Geoffrey Webb. In 1997, the window was restored and a new West window of the Annunciation by Alfred Fisher was installed.

In 1954, Bishop Parker of Northampton commissioned Monsieur Marcel Barbeau to carve a new statue. Marcel used as his model Mme. Marcelle Mandar who has since died in 1964. (In July 1976, her husband, M. Jose Surroca, came on a special mission from France to see the Statue.) On 15th August 1954, this statue was solemnly crowned near the site of the original Shrine on behalf of Pope Pius XII by the Apostolic Delegate, Archbishop O'Hara. The crown made for this occasion was made from 18 carat gold with 118 precious jewels, all gifts, and was fashioned by Mr. W. F. Knight of Wellingborough. It is now only used on special occasions.

Although the chapel has seen some changes over the years, it remains a simple expression of faith in the mystery of the Incarnation as seen through English eyes.

THE HOLY HOUSE AND THE PRIORY

The central object of devotion at Walsingham in former times was the Holy House. This was at a time when statues were virtually unknown. The house was built to remind people of the house of Mary at Nazareth where the Annunciation of the Lord took place and since at that time pilgrimage to the Holy Land was well-nigh impossible, Christians could visit this model instead and reflect here on the Incarnation.

No attempt was made, in building the house, to imitate Palestinian architecture. The house at Nazareth, as far as we can gather, would have been made from the limestone of that area. It would be a small, compact, square structure without windows. The roof would be flat and used for many purposes. Inside the house there would be different levels which would mark out the different functions of the building for the house was accommodation for both man and beast and also workshop.

The Holy House at Walsingham was a simple Anglo-Saxon house. It was a single storey with a pitched roof and was constructed from wood, wattle and daub. A more precise description has not come down to us. It was this house itself which was venerated and through all the changes which were made at the Shrine the Holy House remained undisturbed. In later years, it was enclosed for protection in an outer Chapel of stone which was referred to as the "Novum Opus" or "New Work". The Holy House, which was 23 feet 6 inches long and 12 feet 10 inches wide, stood on a central platform in the centre of the purbeck marble floor of this outer Chapel. In 1511, when Erasmus came, this new work was still not complete for the windows were as yet unglazed. Henry VIII paid for the glass shortly afterwards and the cost was more than £40.

We are indebted to Erasmus for practically the only description of the interior of the Shrine. He says "When you look in you would say that it is the abode of the saints, so brilliantly does it shine on all sides with gems, gold and silver." Votive offerings were constantly being made to the Shrine and Erasmus tells us that there was a Canon in constant attendance by the altar to receive them.

Sometime in the 14th Century, an image was introduced into the Holy House, but it never really replaced the house itself as the centre of the pilgrimage. Erasmus describes the statue as standing beside the altar - "Our Lady stands in the dark at the right side of the altar." What the statue looked like we will never know for certain. Erasmus' description is of "a little image, remarkable neither for size, material, or execution." It would seem reasonable to suppose that the statue which is portrayed on the Priory seal is a fair representation of Our Lady of Walsingham, since this would be a way of distinguishing the Priory. The statue, as far as we know, was burnt at Chelsea in September 1538.

The only other clue we have to what the Shrine looked like is a description of the altar-piece. It seems to have been of gold or gilt and portrayed the Annunciation. The figures of Our Lady and St. Gabriel were vested, in accordance with general custom, in precious cloths. The figures of St. Edward and St. Catherine were on the right and St. Edmund and St. Margaret on the left. At some time there also seems to have been a statue of St. Gabriel in the house which would have been in keeping with the devotion of the Annunciation. The Holy House stood for about four centuries until 1538 when, after being despoiled, it was razed to the ground.

The Priory of the Augustinian Canons was built beside the Holy House on the South side. The first church was built in the mid-12th Century. On the Priory seal there is depicted a Norman church of a cruciform type. The stone for the church was brought from Barnack in Northamptonshire by water to Brookers Dock, traces of which can still be found today just to the North of the Priory site.

After 200 years the church was rebuilt in the Perpendicular style and the whole floor of the church was raised six inches. According to the measurements of William of Worcester who visited the shrine in 1479, the church was 244 feet long and 78 feet wide inside. His measurements have been found accurate by archaeologists. There were two towers, one in the centre and a great one at the west end. The Church must have been similar in this to Wymondham Abbey which can be seen not too far from Walsingham today. There was a central nave and triforium and clerestory with side aisles but no transepts in the usual sense. The church had the usual monastic divisions of choir and nave separated by a screen. Nothing remains today but the remnants of the great East window.

Remains of East window

The rest of the Priory buildings adjoined the church on the South side. There were the cloisters (of which there were arches remaining in the 19th Century), the Chapter House, Dormitory, Refectory (of which there are extensive remains) and the other necessary facilities. There was also a Chapel of St. Lawrence which stood apart some two hundred feet to the East which was said to cover the spot where the Holy House had first been erected. Near this chapel were two wells and a bath which were covered by a wooden shed. We know from Erasmus that there was a bear skin nailed to the roof of this shed. What the importance of this was nobody knows but it must have been of local interest for one of the village inns was named "The Bear". Of the other buildings of the Priory, only the gate-house remains.

David Yaxley, in his <u>A Portrait of Norfolk</u> supports the idea that before the founding of the Shrine much of the settlement of Walsingham probably lay on the East bank of the River Stiffkey around the

Priory Gatehouse and High Street

Parish Church and that the growth of the Shrine and the pilgrimage led to the development of a new town in the 13th Century on the west side of the Priory. Certainly, the rectilinear pattern of the streets and the market places could support this. Fr. Gilbert O.F.M. goes a step further and says that it is possible to trace a geographical pattern in the village which is based on Nazareth so that in all respects this should be England's Nazareth.

OUR LADY AT WALSINGHAM

Our Lady, as she is venerated at Walsingham, is depicted as a simple woman, a mother. She is seated on the throne of Wisdom, in the midst of the Church which is represented by the two pillars symbolic of the Gate of

The Slipper Chapel Statue

Heaven, with seven rings to signify the seven sacraments and the seven gifts of the Holy Spirit. The arched back of the throne reminds us of the rainbow which was set as a sign of God's fidelity to his creation. Our Lady is clothed in the blue of divinity, the white of motherhood and the red of virginity. In her hand she holds a lily-sceptre with three blooms because she was virginal before, during and after the Saviour's birth. As the Woman of the New Creation, the New Eve, she crushes beneath her feet a toadstone, symbolic of the power of evil. As the Queen of Heaven and of England, her Dowry, she is crowned with a Saxon crown. On his mother's knee is the child Jesus who, as the Word of God made Flesh, holds the book of the Gospels. He extends his right arm in a double gesture of blessing and protection of his mother.

Walsingham has never really been the Shrine of Our Lady of Walsingham, but rather the Shrine of Our Lady at Walsingham. There is no competition between Shrines and devotions. Our Lady of Walsingham is Our Lady of Lourdes, of Fatima, of Loreto, of Guadeloupe, of York, Westminster, Ipswich, Mount Grace, Jesmond, Guisborough, Glastonbury, Fernyhalgh, Aylesford. Our Lady of Walsingham is the Virgin Mother of God. The one venerated in this Norfolk village is the homely woman of Nazareth, the woman who listened and believed and who was humble enough to be raised to the dignity of being the mother of God.

There is a special teaching at Walsingham, however. It is this; here we see Mary at Nazareth. The mystery celebrated at Walsingham is the Annunciation. We consider Mary as the handmaid of the Lord and we learn the lesson of humble acceptance of God's will and of co-operation with the Creator. Mary was an ordinary human being who, by God's grace, was able to co-operate in faith with the conception, birth, upbringing and ministry of Jesus. Mary was and still is intimately concerned with God's plan for our salvation expressed in the mission of her child. It was because of this that Mary was with her son from Cana when he began his ministry to the Cross when he completed his work. For Mary too, the road from Nazareth led to Golgotha. Mary was with the Apostles as their support and mainstay as they continued the work of her son and she was with the Church at its birth at Pentecost.

Mary is the faithful follower of the Lord. She is completely dedicated to Christ her son. She is a model for the apostolate, continually presenting Christ the Word to mankind. We can see Mary leading men to her son at Walsingham when she brings them to her English home and there we find that it is not Mary who is at the centre of the Shrine in the Slipper Chapel, but Jesus, Emmanuel, God-with-us in the Eucharist. Mary stands quietly at the side and prays with us, lending support to our prayer with her presence. Our Lady of Walsingham is the woman of concern, the mother of us all who wishes us to share with her in presenting the love of God to the world. Above all, she is Christ-centred.

The woman of Nazareth and Walsingham is the perfect type of the pilgrim church. She is at once the ordinary human being in ordinary circumstances but dominated by the presence of God. Mary is the housewife of Nazareth and at the same time the Seat of Wisdom, extending to us the Logos, the Word made Flesh. She is a citizen of the world and the Queen of Heaven. In Mary at Walsingham, we see what we are and what we shall be. As it says in the Liturgy, in her we see the image and beginning of the church as it is to be perfected in the world to come, here on earth she shines forth as a sign of certain hope and comfort to us, pilgrims until the Lord comes.

In Our Lady at Walsingham we see Mary in the context of Christ's Incarnation of which the Church as his body is an extension. We see her as a mother who is fruitful by the power of the Spirit. We see her as a virgin who is single-minded in her faithfulness to the Lord. We see her as a woman of dedication and we respond by making a dedication of ourselves in the act of pilgrimage. Walsingham, like Nazareth, is an ordinary place inhabited by ordinary people. It is a place which is very much a part of today's world and the needs and ills of the world as well as the many joys are to be found and faced in the prayerful silence of the shrine as they surely were in the house of Joachim and Anne at Nazareth.

CHRONICLE
JOYFUL

The chronicle of Walsingham's history begins in the year 1061 in the reign of Saint Edward the Confessor and five years before the Norman conquest when the widowed Lady of the Manor of Walsingham, Richeldis de Faverches wanted to honour the Mother of God in a special way and so she prayed for guidance. In a dream or vision, Our Lady led Richeldis "in spirit" to the Holy Land, to Nazareth, and there showed her the house in which the Annunciation of the Messiah's birth had taken place.

Mary told Richeldis to take careful note of the measurements of the house and to build one like it at Walsingham to the praise and honour of the Mother of God, so that all who sought her there might find help and so that there should be found a memorial of the great joy of the angelic salutation which heralded our Redemption.

Richeldis called workmen to construct the little house. It was to be 23 feet 6 inches by 12 feet 10 inches. It was made of wood, wattle and daub and no attempt was made to imitate Palestinian architecture. However, a difficulty arose as to where the house should be erected. Richeldis returned to prayer. During the night a heavy dew fell and in the morning in the meadow two spaces of equal area to the new house were found to be quite dry. One of these was beside two wells and Richeldis decided that this was the place to build the house.

The workmen set to work but no matter how hard they tried they could not fix the foundations of the house properly. Night fell and the workmen went home, the task unfinished. Richeldis then spent the night in prayer seeking God's will. The next day the house was found to be completed and standing on the other dry plot at a distance of over two hundred feet from the first site. (At a later date a Chapel of St. Lawrence was built on this spot). As it says in the psalms, "unless the Lord build the house, in vain do the builders labour."

All this was at a time when statues were almost unknown and people visited this house as we today would visit an image. It reminded them of the Holy House in Nazareth, of the Annunciation and of the fact that the Word was made flesh and dwelt among us. The number of pilgrims increased, Walsingham became known as England's Nazareth and eventually a great Priory grew up to serve the many people who wished to share in the joy of Mary at the angelic salutation. Until the time of its destruction in 1538, it was the little wooden house of Richeldis which was the focus for all devotion.

Whatever the truth of the moving of the house and the rest of the legend, these facts seem certain; that Mary herself chose Walsingham as a place in which she wanted to be honoured to the glory of God and that Richeldis de Faverches built a house which was for this purpose and which attracted pilgrims from all England and even abroad for nearly five centuries.

Richeldis' son, Geoffrey, was a child when the Holy House was erected. It seems that he was born about 1061 and he died in 1130. Sometime after his majority (1080) and before 1130 he made a charter giving "To God and to Saint Mary, and to Edwy his chaplain, in perpetuity, the chapel which his mother had founded in Walsingham in honour of Mary ever-Virgin, together with possession of the church of All Hallows in the same village with all its appurtenances in lands, tithes and rents." This was to provide for a religious order to care for the chapel which by now must have been fairly well-established. The date of his death, around 1130, is sometimes offered as a possible later date for the actual founding of the Shrine.

The present writer has chosen to accept the traditional date of 1061, but there has been considerable discussion about the date of the foundation of the shrine and the arguments for both sides have been very complicated. For a fuller discussion, the reader is referred to A. H. Bond, The Walsingham Story Through 900 years (which supports the 1061 date) and J. C. Dickinson, The Shrine of Our Lady of Walsingham (which favours a later date). Only a brief outline of each argument will be attempted here.

The date 1061 comes from the Pynson Ballad published in about 1496 by Richard Pynson, printer to King Henry VII which says:

"Of this chapel see here the foundation
Builded the year of Christ's incarnation
A thousand complete sixty and one
The time of Saint Edward king of this region."

A note in a 15th Century Book of Hours in Cambridge University Library also confirms 1061 as the date of the foundation of the Shrine.

As evidence in favour of this date we may note that Geoffrey de Faverches confirmed his mother's foundation in an undated charter preserved in the British Museum. This must have been before 1130 by which time he was dead since it is recorded that in that year William of Houghton married the (un-named) widow of Geoffrey and took custody of her son (also un-named).

If we follow the ballad, Geoffrey must have been born before 1061, since his mother, Richeldis, was herself a widow at the time of her inspiration. In this case, the charter must be dated between the attainment of his majority around 1080 and his death around 1130. That he should have lived for about 70 years is not beyond possibility.

In the charter, Geoffrey mentions the chapel founded by his mother and its living as possessed by Edwy, his chaplain, before the journey which he made to Jerusalem. Geoffrey may be referring to the First Crusade which was preached in 1095. This would bring the foundation of the shrine before this date.

The date of circa 1153 comes from the date of the foundation of the Priory of the Augustinian Canons which, according to the list of Priors preserved in the British Museum, was in or about 1153. The earliest date Dickinson will allow is 1130 when Geoffrey de Faverches probably died. He takes the sequence of events as the ballad records them as accurate and therefore sticks to the story that Richeldis was a widow and that she founded a chapel of Our Lady before the Priory was founded. He identifies Richeldis with the un-named widow of Geoffrey married by William of Houghton in 1130. He also makes the point that the Doomsday Book makes no reference to an earlier Richeldis. The Geoffrey who made the charter then becomes the son of Richeldis and the late Geoffrey. This charter was confirmed by Roger, Earl of Clare sometime between 1152 - 56 and thus the Shrine was founded before this date. The journey to Jerusalem which Geoffrey had made may then be identified with the Second Crusade which was held between 1147 - 48. This may have been the inspiration behind the Shrine in which case would have been founded between 1148 - 52.

The difference between the two theories may briefly be summarised thus:

The common facts are:

1. that there was a Geoffrey de Faverches who was dead by 1130 when William of Houghton had leave to marry his widow.

2. that Geoffrey had a son,

3. that between 1152 and 1156 Geoffrey's charter was confirmed.

4. that in 1153 the Priory was founded to care for the existing Shrine.

5. that in 1199 there was one named Richard, son of Geoffrey still alive.

In the 1061 theory, Geoffrey de Faverches was the son of Richeldis who founded the Shrine. In the c1153 theory, he is the husband of Richeldis. In the 1061 theory, he makes his charter sometime between 1080 and 1130. In the c1153 theory, it is his son, Geoffrey II who makes the charter sometime before 1152. In the 1061 theory, the 1153 date of the founding of the Priory means that Geoffrey de Faverches' intentions as outlined in his charter were carried out by his son. In the c1153 theory they were carried out person-ally. In the 1061 theory, the Richard who is alive in 1199 is the son of the original Geoffrey de Faverches. In the c1153 theory he is the grandson. Thus the difference between the theories is that of a generation which, in the 1061 theory, is supplied before the original Geoffrey de Faverches and, in the c1153 theory, after his son.

In any event, in 1153 a Priory of Augustinian Canons was founded and the first Prior, Ralph, took up office. He was Prior until 1173. Confirmation of Geoffrey de Faverches' gifts to the Priory was made to William Turbus, Bishop of Norwich by Robert de Brucurt in 1169. Robert makes it known to the Bishop that he grants all the possessions which the Priory held on the day when Geoffrey set out for Jerusalem.

By 1224 there must have been many pilgrims coming to Walsingham for in that year a hospice for poor pilgrims was founded by William de Bec at Billingford which is on the way from Norwich. Two years later Walsingham received royal approval when the first King of England came as a pilgrim. Henry III is recorded as coming in 1226 and again in at least nine subsequent years. (1229, -32, -38, -42, -45, -48, -51, -66, -72). On the Feast of the Assumption of Our Lady in 1241, Henry sent an offering of 3,000 tapers to light the Shrine.

The Priory grew in proportion to the fame of the little Shrine. About 1280, extensions were made to the property and additional chapels of St. Lawrence (on the first site of the Holy House) and St. Nicholas were built. The Priory was still not all that wealthy for when the Archbishop of Canterbury, Archbishop Peckham, made his visitation in 1280, the Priory was heavily in debt.

In the following year, 1281, King Edward I came on pilgrimage. He had come in thanksgiving. He had been playing chess with a knight in a vaulted chamber when suddenly, without reason, he rose and went away, where-upon a huge stone which would have crushed him had he remained, fell on the very spot where he had been sitting. He attributed his escape from this danger to the favour of Our Lady of Walsingham. Edward was back again in 1289 and in November 1295 he sent valuable gifts of jewels and wax. On Candlemas Day, 2nd February 1296, the little Chapel was the setting for the sealing of an alliance on behalf of Edward I and the Earl of Flanders. On the same day, one year later, Edward returned to offer Our Lady a gold brooch set with a cameo which had formed part of the Scottish treasure won by him at Edinburgh. The year 1298 saw Edward there again. He made a practice of always visiting Our Lady of Walsingham before an important event or campaign.

In 1314 one of the most famous of the miracles associated with the Shrine occurred. A knight, Sir Ralph Boutetort, in full armour and on horseback, was being pursued by a cruel enemy and was in grave danger of being taken near the Priory. He made directly for a little wicket gate on the North side of the grounds which normally it would have been impossible for him to pass through. However, he invoked Our Lady's help and immediately found himself and his horse within the sanctuary. Erasmus records a copper plaque depicting the Knight's escape which was affixed to the gate. The gate became known as the Knight's Gate and a reconstruction now stands on the site. The street opposite takes its name - Knight Street - from this incident.

In 1315 King Edward II came as a pilgrim and the continuity of the Kings of England as pilgrims was furthered by his successor, Edward III coming in 1328. Nor were the English kings the only royal pilgrims. Queen Isabella of France visited Walsingham in 1332 and the municipal records of King's Lynn tell us that it cost the town 20 shillings to provide bread for her as she passed through.

By this time the number of pilgrims had increased tremendously. The routes to Walsingham were well established and marked with wayside crosses and chapels. The last of these, St. Catherine's or the Slipper Chapel, was built just over a mile outside the village. The earliest date given for its foundation is 1338, but it could have been as late as 1380.

The increase in pilgrims also brought a new religious order to Walsingham. In February 1347 King Edward III gave permission for a Franciscan Friary to be founded and this was licensed by Pope Clement VI on 28th September of that year. Needless to say, there was great opposition from the Canons at the Priory who feared that their revenue would suffer. The Friars won the day and in 1351 they obtained permission to enclose the existing road into

Friary Ruins

Walsingham which came in at the South West corner of the Friday Market. They probably caused the present Fakenham road to be constructed at that time.

The popularity of the Shrine continued and as a mark of this Edward III returned in 1361 and in 1364 King David of Scotland was allowed safe conduct through England with an escort from the King in order that he could make the pilgrimage. In 1383 Richard II and his Queen came. It was in Richard's time that the title "Our Lady's Dowry" was officially accepted for England. When we speak of Kings visiting Walsingham we must remember that we are not just speaking of individuals, wherever the King went, the whole court followed and so there must have been hundreds in these retinues. It is said that on one occasion even Parliament came and met in the Common Place.

As the years passed, royalty continued to favour Walsingham with Henry V coming in 1421, Queen Johanna, the widow of Henry IV in 1427 and Henry VI in 1447.

The story of the Shrine is not one of untarnished virtue. With so much popularity, there was bound to be some abuse and it seems that the traders in the village were not wholly scrupulous. John of Amundesham relates that in the year 1431 "after Easter, there was a great fire in Walsingham Parva, which consumed four of the inns in that town; by whom or through what cause, this misfortune happened, no mortal knew, except that it might be from revenge for the excessive and unjust extortionate charges which the persons living in those inns had extracted from the pilgrims for their victuals."

One of the Walsingham Inns - The Oxford Stores

All was not well at the Priory in these years either. Shortly after the fire, in 1448, another licence was granted to the Priory to acquire lands to augment the revenue of the house because the lack of money was such that the services of the church were hardly able to be celebrated properly. Better times were to come for by 1500 the Priory owned 18 of the inns in the village.

In May 1469 Edward IV and his Queen came. In 1479 the measurements of the Shrine and the Priory church were recorded on the visit of William of Worcester. He found the Holy House to measure 23 feet 6 inches by 12 feet 10 inches and the inside of the great church he measured as 136 paces by 36 paces. In 1487 Henry VII came in thanksgiving for the quelling of the Lambert Simnel rebellion and he left his banner in the Chapel as a memorial.

About this time the Shrine was celebrated in a ballad. One date for its composition in 1465 but a more probable date would be 1496. It is usually referred to as the Pynson Ballad because it was published by Richard Pynson, printer to Henry VII. What seems to be the only extant copy is preserved in the Pepys Library of Magdalene College, Cambridge.

It is here given in full with the spellings modernised.

Of this chapel see here the foundation
Builded the year of Christ's incarnation
A thousand complete sixty and one
The time of Saint Edward king of this region.

Behold and see ye ghostly folks all
Which to this place have devotion
When ye to our Lady asking succour call
Desiring here her help in your tribulation
Of this her chapel ye may see the foundation
If ye will this table overse and read
How by miracle it was founded indeed.

A noble widow sometime lady of this town
Called Rychold in living full virtuous
Desired of our Lady a petition
Her to honour with some work bounteous
This blessed virgin and lady most gracious
Granted her petition as I shall after tell
Unto her worship to edify this chapel.

In spirit our Lady to Nazareth her led
And showed her the place where Gabriel her grette
Lo daughter consider to her our Lady said
Of this place take thou surely the mette
Another like this at Walsingham thou set
Unto my laud and singular honour
All that me seek there shall find succour.

Where shall be had in a memorial
The great joy of my salutation
First of my joys ground and original
Root of mankind's gracious redemption
When Gabriel gave to me relation
To be a mother through humility
And God's son conceive in virginity.

This vision showed thrice to this devout woman
In mind well she marked length and brede
She was full glad and thanked our Lady then
Of her great grace never destitute in need
This foresaid house she thought to speed
Called to her artificers full wise
This chapel to forge as our Lady did devise.

All this a meadow wet with drops celestial
And with silver dew sent from on high adown
Except the twain places chosen above all
Where neither moisture nor dew might be found
This was the first prognostication
How this our new Nazareth here should stand
Builded like the first in the Holy Land.

When it was all formed then had she great doubt
Where it should be set and in what manner place
Inasmuch twain places were found out
Tokened with miracle of our Lady's grace
That is to say twain quadrates of equal space
As the fleece of Gideon in the wet being dry
Assigned by miracle of holy maid Mary.

The widow thought it most likely of congruence
This house on the first soil to build and arear
Of this who list to have experience
A chapel of Saint Lawrence standeth now there
Fast by twain wells experience doth lere
There she thought to have set this chapel
Which was begun by our Lady's counsel.

The carpenters began to set the fundament
This heavenly house to arear up on high
But soon their works showed inconvenient
For no piece with other would agree
     with geometry
Then were they all sorry and full of agony
That they could not ken neither measure
   nor mark
To join together their own proper work.

They went to rest and laid all things on side
As they on their mistress had a commandment
She thought that our Lady that first was her guide
Would convey this work after her own intent
Her men to rest as for that night she sent
And prayed our Lady with devout exclamation
And as she had begun to perform that habitation.

All night the widow remained in this prayer
Our blessed Lady with heavenly ministries
Herself being here chief artificer
Areared this said house with angels hands
And not only reared it but set it there it is
That is two hundred foot and more in distance
From the first place books make remembrance.

Early when the artificers came to their travail
Of this said chapel to have made an end
They found each part conjoined sans fail
Better than they could conceive it in mind
Thus each man home again did wynde
And this holy matron thanked our Lady
Of her great grace showed here specially.

And sith here our Lady hath shewed many miracle
Innumerable now here for to express
To such as visit this her habitacle
Ever like new to them that call her in distress
Four hundred year and more the chronicle to witness
Hath endured this notable pilgrimage
Where grace is daily showed to men of every age.

Many sick been here cured by
    our Lady's might
Dead again revived of this is no doubt
Lame made whole and blind restored
    to sight
Mariners vexed with tempest safe
    to port brought
Deaf wound and lunatic that hither
    have fought
And also lepers here recovered have be
By our Lady's grace of their infirmity.

Folk that of fiends have had encumbrance
And of wicked spirits also much vexation
Here be delivered from every such chance
And souls greatly vexed with ghostly
    temptation
Lo here the chief solace against all
    tribulation
To all that be sick bodily or ghostly
Calling to our Lady devoutly.

Therefore every pilgrim give your
  attendance
Our Lady here to serve with humble
  affection
Yourself ye apply to do her pleasance
Remembering the great joy of her
  annunciation
Therewith conceiving this brief
  compilation
Though it halt in metre and eloquence
It is here written to do her reverence.

All lettered that will have more intelligence
Of the foundation of this chapel here
If ye will ask books shall you enchance
More clearly to understand this foresaid matter
To you shall declare the chronicler
All circumstance by a noble process
How old chroniclers of this bear witness.

O England great cause thou hast glad for to be
Compared to the land of promise Sion
Thou attainest by grace to stand in that degree
Through this glorious Lady's supportation
To be called in every realm and region
The Holy Land Our Lady's Dowry
Thus art thou named of old antiquity.

And this is the cause as it appeareth by likliness
In thee is builded new Nazareth a mansion
To the honour of the heavenly empress
And of her most glorious salutation
When Gabriel said at old Nazareth ave
This joy here daily remembered for to be.

O gracious lady glory of Jerusalem
Cypress of Sion and joy of Israel
Rose of Jericho and star of Bethlehem
O glorious lady our asking not repel
In mercy all women ever thou dost excel
Therefore blessed lady grant thou thy great grace
To all that thee devoutly visit in this place.

Amen.

The sixteenth century came upon Walsingham without any hint of what it was to bring. In 1509 we learn of a bequest benefitting a hermit living at the Slipper Chapel. In January 1511, Henry VIII made an offering to our Lady of £1 3s 4d. It seems that this offering was made in person by the King on his first visit to Walsingham in thanksgiving for the birth of a son, Prince Henry. Tradition says that he walked barefoot to the Shrine from

East Barsham Manor

East Barsham Manor and offered in the Shrine a valuable necklace. In June of that year the exchequer books of Henry VIII record part payment for glazing Our Lady's chapel at Walsingham and the following year record a payment of over £23 for the completion of the work.

Erasmus also visited the Shrine in 1511 and he mentions that at that time the windows of the outer chapel around the Holy House were unglazed and that the winds from the nearby sea howled through. Erasmus seemed to have mixed feelings towards the Shrine. On the one hand he based his satirical Pilgrimage of True Devotion on the experience and on the other hand he wrote a beautiful prayer to Our Lady of Walsingham which is still used by pilgrims today:

"O Alone of all women, Mother and Virgin, Mother most happy, Virgin most pure, now we sinful as we are, come to see thee who are all pure. We salute thee, we honour thee as how we may with our humble offerings; may thy Son grant us, that imitating thy most holy manners, we also, by the grace of the Holy Ghost may deserve spiritually to conceive the Lord Jesus in our inmost soul, and once conceived never to lose him. Amen."

In 1514 after the victory of Flodden Field, Queen Katherine of Aragon came to Walsingham in fulfilment of her vow. On 16th September she announced her intention of doing so to the king: "And with this I make an end, praying God to send you home shortly, for without this no joy here can be accomplished; and for the same I pray and now go to our Lady at Walsingham that I promised so long ago to see." Her fidelity was shortly to be sadly betrayed and in this betrayal our Lady's Shrine was to suffer with so many others.

Cardinal Wolsey came to Walsingham to pray for a return to good health. This was in 1517. He was the last Cardinal to visit the Shrine until Cardinal Bourne led the National Pilgrimage in 1934. Wolsey made a gift to the Shrine in 1528 which was useful because revenue was once again dwindling. The grant of the Priory of Flitcham to Walsingham expressly states of the shrine "that the universal devotion by which it was first sustained is now cooled by the perverse reviling of some, and the pestiferous preaching of others."

SORROWFUL

The end of Walsingham's Shrine was not far away. The King's Commissioners made straight for Walsingham with the Act of Supremacy and the Prior and Canons became one of the first religious houses in England to submit when they signed the Oath on 18th September 1534. By this act they recognised the marriage of Henry and Anne Boleyn and the right of succession of their children. They also acknowledged Henry to be head of the Church in England and renounced the supremacy of the Pope.

Then came the suppression of the religious houses. Walsingham escaped the first dissolution being among the greater monasteries but its turn came. An interesting letter concerning the dissolution of the Priory has been preserved. It is from Richard Southwell to Cromwell. "It may please your good lordship to be advertised that Sir Thomas Lestrange and Mr. Hoges, according unto the sequestration delegate unto them, have been at Walsingham, and there sequestered all such money, plate, jewels, and stuff, as there was invented and found. Among other things the same Sir Thomas Lestrange and Mr. Hoges did there find a secret privy place within the house, where no Canon nor any other of the house did ever enter, as they say, in which there were instruments, pots, bellows, phials of such strange colours as the like none of us had seen with poises and other things to sort and divide gold and silver, nothing there wanting that should belong to the art of multiplying. Of all which they desired me by letters to advertise you, and also that from the Saturday at nigh till the Sunday next following was offered at there now being 33s 3d over and beside wax." The description of the instruments of the art of multiplying (alchemy) could well refer to the materials for making the pilgrim badges.

In July the Royal Commissioners closed the Shrine, and on the 14th July 1538 the revered statue was taken away. It arrived in London on the 18th when this letter was written by John Hussee to Lord Lisle: "This day our late lady of Walsingham was brought to Lambeth, where was both my lord Chancellor and my lord Privy Seal (Cromwell) with many virtuous prelates, but there was offered neither ob' nor candle, What shall become of her is not determined." It seems as though the statue was burned along with others at Chelsea in September 1538 in the presence of Cromwell. There is little to support the tradition that the statue was secretly preserved. On 4th August 1538, the Priory was handed over to the Commissioners. All that was valuable was looted and the Holy House built by Richeldis was burned to the ground. In September of that year there is a final brief entry in King Henry VIII's book of payments which speaks volumes: "For the King's candle before our Lady of Walsingham and to the Prior there for his salary. Nil."

However, Our Lady of Walsingham was not so easily displaced. On 20th January 1539, Roger Townsend writes to Cromwell:

"Please it your good lordship to be advertised that there was a poor woman of Wells beside Walsingham, that imagined a false tale of a miracle to be done by the image of our Lady that was at Walsingham sith the same was brought from thence to London; and upon the trial thereof, by my examination from one person to another, to the number of six persons, and at last came to her that she was the reporter thereof, and to be the very author of the same, as far forth as my conscience and perceiving could lead me; I committed her therefore to the ward of the constables of Walsing-ham. The next day after, being market day there, I caused her to be set in the stocks in the morning, and at about nine of the clock when the said market was fullest of people, with a paper set about her head written with these words upon the same, "A reporter of false tales." was set in a cart and so carried about the market-sted, and other streets in the town, staying in divers places where most people assembled, young people and boys of the town casting snowballs at her. This done and executed was brought to the stocks again and there sat till the market was ended. This was her penance; for I knew no law otherwise to punish her but by discretion; trusting it shall be a warning to other light persons in such wise to order themself. How be it I cannot perceive, but the said Image is not yet out of some of their heads,"

At least the means of punishment employed here was less drastic than that used to silence the voice of dissent two years earlier when two men from the village were executed for speaking against the changes at the Priory. Nicholas Mileham, the sub-Prior of the monastery, and George Guisborough, a layman, were hanged, drawn and quartered on 30th May 1537 in a field overlooking the village which is still known today as the Martyrs' Field.

At the Dissolution the Priory was sold to Sir Thomas Sidney for £90. He had been commissioned by the townsfolk to buy it on their behalf and then he refused to hand it over. In the reign of Edward VI (1547 - 1553) it was given to Sir Thomas Gresham and then it descended to Robert, Earl of Leicester. By the time Queen Elizabeth I visited Walsingham Priory, it was known as "Mr. Sidney's". This was in 1578.

At that time there were only three Catholic families left in Walsingham. On her visit to Mr. Sidney's the Queen was probably accompanied by Sir Philip Howard. He was to end his life on 19th October 1595 in the Tower of London as a martyr for his faith.

Modern photograph of House and East window

The Walsingham Lament which could have been based on the experience of his visit to the ruined Priory is often attributed to him although his authorship is now disputed.

In the wracks of Walsingham
Whom should I choose
But the Queen of Walsingham
To be guide to my muse?

Then thou Prince of Walsingham,
Grant me to frame
Bitter plaints to rue thy wrong
Bitter woe for thy name.

Bitter was it, oh to see
The seely sheep
Murdered by the ravening wolves,
While the shepherds did sleep.

Bitter was it, oh to view
The sacred vine
Whiles the gardeners played all close
Rooted up by the swine.

Bitter, bitter, oh to behold
The grass to grow
Where the walls of Walsingham
So stately did show.

Such were the works of Walsingham
While she did stand
Such are the wracks as now do show
of that holy land!

Level, level with the ground
The towers do lie,
Which with their golden glittering tops
Pierced once to the sky.

Where were gates no gates are now;
The ways unknown
Where the press of peers did pass
While her fame far was blown.

Owls do shriek where the sweetest hymns
Lately were sung;
Toads and serpents hold their dens
Where the Palmers did throng.

Weep, weep, O Walsingham
Whose days are nights,
Blessings turned to blasphemies,
Holy deeds to despites.

Sin is where Our Lady sat,
Heaven turned is to hell,
Satan sits where our Lord did sway,
Walsingham, oh farewell!

The following centuries saw Walsingham sleeping, returning once again to the life of a small village. The Priory, all that remained of the great Shrine, was passed from hand to hand. In 1650 Robert, Earl of Leicester, conveyed the Priory to Henry English and others and in 1660 they sold the property to the Bishop of Rochester, John Warner, who bequeathed it to his sister, Mrs. Lee. (Her family assumed the name Lee Warner.) In 1756 the Lee Warner family also acquired the Manor of Walsingham when Henry Lee Warner bought it from Norborne Berkely, Lord Botetort. The Priory is still in the hands of the same family for the present owners, the Gurney family, are descended from the Lee Warners.

Although the Shrine had gone and the Priory was in secular hands it seems that Our Lady of Walsingham was never totally forgotten. There was a tradition that Catholics used to visit the Slipper Chapel (which was by now a barn) where they would kneel and pray. It is possible to trace this back as far as 1800 and it would not be beyond the bounds of possibility for the practice to have continued beyond this date.

GLORIOUS

The 19th Century was to see a re-awakening of Walsingham. In 1854 Canon James Lee Warner excavated part of the site of the Priory and determined the position of the Holy House. In 1894 Charlotte Boyd began negotiations to buy the Slipper Chapel. Later that year she was received into the Catholic Church. In 1897 work was begun in May on the

Slipper Chapel before restoration

restoration of the Slipper Chapel and in the same year, on 19th August, a statue of Our Lady modelled on Our Lady of Cosmedin, carved in Oberammergau and blessed by Pope Leo XIII in February was enshrined in a new chapel built at the parish church of the Annunciation in King's Lynn. The new chapel based on the Holy House of Loreto was to be the restored Shrine of Our Lady of Walsingham. At this time, there were no Catholics living in Walsingham itself. ⁻

On 20th August 1897, the day after the dedication of the new shrine, the parish priest of King's Lynn led what is counted as the first pilgrimage of modern times to Walsingham. He was accompanied by the Master of the Guild of Ransom, Fr. Philip Fletcher, and the Prior of Downside, Fr. Edmund Ford O.S.B. The Eastern Daily Press on 21st August 1897 gave the following account of the proceedings:

"The advent of the pilgrims to Walsingham was watched for in the rain by the inhabitants. However, on the arrival of the 12.18 train, some excited children rushed from the station with the news. "They've come, they've come!" and after a short interval a procession of some forty or fifty persons headed by a crucifix, flanked with burning tapers and led by a priest wended their way to the way-side Chapel, where a short private service was held, after which the doors were thrown open and the public admitted.

The beautiful little chapel was quickly crowded but the proceedings were of a very brief but devout character, the party wending their way back for refreshments to the Black Lion Hotel where a luncheon had been provided.

After this the party dispersed to visit the Abbey, Church and Friary and left by the 3.55 train expressing a hope to visit the old town again next year."

As the years tick away we see the shrine becoming more and more consolidated. In 1906 Charlotte Boyd died. In 1921 Fr. Alfred Hope Patten was appointed as the Vicar of Walsingham and in the ancient Parish Church he set up a statue of Our Lady of Walsingham and began and encouraged the devotion which still continues to flourish today. In the following year the Priory (now called the Abbey) came into the hands of the Gurney family who are related to the Lee Warners. They still hold the property today. The little shrine which Fr. Hope Patten had set up became increasingly popular among Anglo-Catholics in the Church of England and in 1931 a new shrine was built just outside the Priory walls at the corner of Knight Street. This shrine contained a modern Holy House based (like the one at King's Lynn) on the Shrine at Loreto. By 1938 an elaborate shrine Church had been built around the Holy House which today draws thousands of pilgrims and is the scene of many graces and answers to prayer.

In 1933 Mgr. Laurence Youens was consecrated Bishop of Northampton and at his installation he vowed that one of the chief aims of his episcopate would be to restore devotion to Our Lady at Walsingham. In this year a new statue designed by Professor Tristram from the details shown of the Priory seal was enthroned and on the Feast of the Assumption Bishop Youens celebrated the first public mass in the Slipper Chapel for 400 years.

Bishop Youens after the first Mass in the Slipper Chapel, 15th August 1934

On the next Sunday, 19th August, Cardinal Bourne became the first Cardinal since Thomas Wolsey to come as a pilgrim to Walsingham. He led 12,000 people in the first National Pilgrimage to the Slipper Chapel which was then designated by the Hierarchy of England and Wales with the approval of the Pope to be the National Shrine of Our Lady for England.

The account of this event (commemorated by a panel in the pulpit of Westminster Cathedral) which was written by the Cardinal's biographer, Ernest Oldmeadow, is worth quoting in full.

"The first Catholic pilgrimage to Walsingham of our times seems to have been planned in the belief that pilgrims in the twentieth century are even tougher than were their fifteenth century forebears. Too much was crowded into one day. London pilgrims had to make their way to Liverpool Street station before the tube-railways and omnibuses began to operate, which meant for some of them a rising with the lark and a walk of some miles. After more than three hours in the train, there had to be a high-speed rush to St. John's, that noble church, of cathedral dimensions, which Henry, Duke of Norfolk, gave to Norwich. There the Archbishop of Cardiff celebrated Pontifical High Mass, in the presence of Cardinal Bourne, and the Bishop of Northampton preached.

With no time for a peep at Norwich Cathedral, the pilgrims panted to the old Blackfriars' Hall, now secularized, for a quick and cold meal. Thence they sped back to the station for seventy minutes more in a train. Arriving at Walsingham, the elderly and those who, like Hamlet, were "fat and scant of breath", learned that they had barely two hours to walk to the Slipper Chapel and back, to witness a very long procession, to hear a sermon by Fr. Vernon Johnson and to assist at Benediction. The result was that hundreds of pilgrims had to stampede back to the station before the ceremonies were over. They got away from Walsingham at six o'clock and once more saw Liverpool Street at eleven. Later pilgrimages were better managed. Norwich was left out, and passengers could, on some occasions, detrain near the Slipper Chapel itself.

"The Cardinal, of course, was not allowed to undergo this physical ordeal. He went to Norwich betimes; and, after High Mass in that city, he was driven to the Slipper Chapel in his own car. Cars indeed, made the strongest contrast between the old Walsingham pilgrimages and the new. Ranging from the humblest two-seaters to the hugest chars-a-bancs, they filled a vast park above the meadow. Enamelled with all the colours of the rainbow, and with all their glass and bright metal flashing back the August sunshine, these hundreds of cars smote the eye like Kingsor's gaudy garden, sprawling out along the parched green hillside. And it was a car which made the most striking innovation of all. When the Bishop of Northampton, under a canopy, bore the Blessed Sacrament away from the Slipper Chapel to the temporary altar in the meadow where the multitude stood waiting, he was closely followed by a car, which its driver, Mgr. George Coote, skilfully piloted at a foot-pace down a narrow lane and up a rough

Cardinal Bourne in his car leading the 1934 Pilgrimage

slope of tussocky grass. In it was the Cardinal, who could not otherwise have reached the place of Benediction. Yet despite this touch of modernity, the very long procession was one of unworldly beauty. Processions in church, or along paved ways, such as Cardinal Bourne had often seen on great Feasts and at Eucharistic Congresses, can keep close formation and are somewhat stiff. Up the uneven slope in Houghton meadow the bevies of young girls, some in white, some in blue, and the many thousands of laics and clerics with their hundreds of banners, took a serpentine path which gave them an undulant and most vital movement. In church, the almost static draperies and robes of a procession maintain their prim folds. At Houghton a kindly breeze ruffled the white and blue dresses, as it ruffles ripe corn, and it lovingly spread out the veils upon the warm air. In church the light remains fixed and hard. At Houghton no two moments of illumination were the same; because Pilgrimage Sunday was a hide-and-seek day of sun and cloud." (E. Oldmeadow, <u>Francis Cardinal Bourne</u>, 1944).

1934 also saw the erection by Bishop Youens of a Guild of Our Lady of Walsingham, which was to further the cause of the Shrine. This flourishes today as the Walsingham Association. In 1935 a priest was appointed to

Walsingham for the first time since the Reformation when Fr. Bruno Scott James became Priest-Custodian of the Shrine. During his office the Shrine continued to blossom. In June 1937 a great Children's Pilgrimage took place and the rain poured down for it. In November of that year the habit of the sons of Saint Francis was once again seen in the streets of Walsingham for then the Franciscans returned on the invitation of Bishop Youens to open two hostels for poor pilgrims, St. Francis's for men and St. Clare's for women.

Fr. Bruno Scott James and Capuchin Friars

Fr. Bruno Scott James was responsible for some major developments at the Slipper Chapel. A much-needed sacristy was provided and an additional Chapel of the Holy Ghost was built to provide an additional altar for the many Masses which were being celebrated at the Shrine. On 8th September 1938 the two chapels were consecrated by Bishop Youens and the auxiliary in Westminster, Bishop Myers.

1938 also saw the first National Pilgrimage of Catholic Youth. On 2nd July, Cardinal Hinsley marked the 400th anniversary of the desecration of the Shrine by leading 10,000 Catholic young people in a pilgrimage of reparation and of prayer for peace. Pontifical High Mass was sung outside the Slipper Chapel by Bishop Myers and a procession was formed to the

Consecration of Slipper Chapel, 8th September 1938

ruins of the Priory which were opened to the pilgrims by permission of Lady Gurney. The Cardinal presented her with a bouquet of flowers as he entered the grounds and the procession moved to the site of the Holy House where the Cardinal lay a sheaf of lilies. All knelt in prayer for a few moments and the procession left. As the pilgrims departed, Lady Gurney was seen to place her own flowers beside the Cardinal's. Afterwards the Credo was sung in the Common Place and in the evening the beacon in the Common Place was fired and there was a torchlight procession to the Lourdes hymn.

The total number of pilgrims during 1938 was more than 50,000 and with so many people coming to Walsingham the need was felt for some sort of organization to co-ordinate events. In that year, therefore, the Bishop of Northampton founded the Walsingham Catholic Bureau to help anyone wishing to come on pilgrimage. Mr. Claude Fisher was the first Honorary Secretary and worked for over 40 years in the service of pilgrims in the Pilgrim Bureau.

Then came the War and Walsingham became part of a restricted zone which meant that there could be no pilgrimages. In April 1944, Fr. Bruno Scott James left Walsingham and Fr. Roberts, the parish priest of nearby

Fakenham (in which parish Walsingham lay) stepped in as Priest-Custodian. On 17th May 1945 the first Mass since the Reformation on the site of the Priory's High Altar was offered at a pilgrimage of American Servicemen who were stationed in East Anglia.

The War ended and in 1948 the Franciscans left Walsingham. In that year a great cross-carrying pilgrimage took place as an act of reparation for the War and as a prayer for peace. Fourteen groups of about 30 men each walked from places as far North as Middlesbrough and as far South as Canterbury. Each group carried a heavy wooden cross for over 200 miles and arrived outside Walsingham on 15th July. The campfires of the men burned in a circle around the village through the night as the men kept vigil in prayer before their crosses and at daybreak on the 16th they processed into Walsingham. This was also the day of the annual pilgrimage of the Union of Catholic Mothers. Pontifical High Mass was sung at the open-air altar at the Slipper Chapel and in the afternoon the 14 crosses were solemnly borne into the village led by Cardinal Griffin, Bishop Parker of Northampton and many others. At the Priory site there was the blessing of the sick and Solemn Benediction. It was on this occasion that Cardinal Griffin dedicated England to the Immaculate Heart of Mary. The crosses now form a permanent Way of the Cross in the grounds of the Slipper Chapel.

Since about the same time there has been a cross carrying pilgrimage every year formed by students from the universities. The members of Student Cross spend Holy Week walking to Walsingham and after carrying out the solemn ceremonies of Good Friday and Holy Saturday, they celebrate the joy of the Resurrection with the "Holy Trot" around the village carrying the flower-decked crosses and then with country dancing in the Friday Market on Easter Sunday morning. Their annual visit has become one of Walsingham's most cherished traditions.

Another group who always walk to Walsingham are the men of the Guild of Our Lady of Ransom who come from London each September to pray for England's return to the Faith and to raise money for poor parishes throughout the country.

To get back to the year 1948, when the Franciscans left Walsingham, Fr. Gerard Langley was appointed priest there. During this time the building of a temporary church for the Catholics of the area was under way. In 1949, Fr. Langley was moved and Fr. Roberts came from Fakenham to replace him. At this time, Bishop Parker of Northampton was working towards making Walsingham a parish in its own right. Fr. Roberts saw the Church of the Annunciation completed and on 2nd July 1950 Bishop Parker officiated at the opening. In 1951 Fr. Roberts was moved to Norwich and Fr. Gerard Hulme was appointed to Walsingham as parish priest and Priest-Custodian of the Shrine.

Fr. Gerard Hume in 1958 looks on as the Trinity is positioned on the West front of the Slipper Chapel. Next to Fr. Hume is Miss Agnes Perowne, Sacristan.

Bishop Parker was back in Walsingham again in 1953, this time to bless the new East window of the Slipper Chapel which was erected to commemorate the recent definition of the dogma of Our Lady's Assumption. In the Marian Year of 1954 Walsingham was accorded the rare privilege of having the Shrine statue crowned on behalf of the Pope. The coronation was carried out by the Apostolic Delegate, Archbishop O'Hara in the Priory grounds in the presence of 15,000 people. In the same year Cardinal Griffin

Benediction at the Slipper Chapel outside altar, 15th August 1954

presented a copy of the new statue to the Shrine of Saint James at Compostella in Spain.

1961, the 900th anniversary of the founding of the Shrine, was marked with a Pontifical High Mass offered by Bishop Parker on 20th August with a congregation of some 7,000 pilgrims. This was also the year when the excavation of part of the Priory site was carried out under the auspices of the Royal Archaeological Society. The South and East footings of the "Novum Opus" and part of its North porch were uncovered and the mortar base for the floor surrounding the central platform where the Holy House stood was seen. The Society published a full report of their findings which confirmed the excavation of Canon Lee Warner in 1854 in determining the centre of the original pilgrimage.

Another new development in the Shrine's story took place in February 1968 when Bishop Grant gave the Shrine into the care of the priests of the Society of Mary, the Marist Fathers, and Fr. Roland Connelly s.m. arrived in Walsingham as Administrator and Priest-Custodian of the Shrine. The

Fr. Connelly, the Apostolic Delegate, Archbishop Enrici with Sr. Madeleine and Sr. Celine, 4th September 1971

Marists were also given care of the parish of the Annunciation which extends for some 120 square miles. Fr. Walter Symes s.m. was the first Marist parish priest. In that year 15,000 organised pilgrims were recorded.

Like Fr. Bruno Scott James before him, Fr. Connelly had to provide for the increasing flow of pilgrims. A Pilgrim Centre was built at the Slipper Chapel designed by the late Mr. Donovan Purcell of Norwich and built by Fisher's of Fakenham to provide the necessary facilities for essential refreshments, toilets and a repository. It was completed in 1970.

One of the "Founding Fathers" in the restoration of Walsingham was Mr. Claude Fisher who at one time was the only Catholic in the village. For over 40 years Mr. Fisher served the Shrine and the countless pilgrims and in 1972 the Pope made him a Knight of St. Gregory for his services to Walsingham. Claude continued to be a father-figure for the Pilgrim Bureau until his death on 14th May 1985. A talented photographer, he left a tremendous legacy in the archives which he built up. 1972 was also the year when the first Pilgrimage of the Sick took place. There were over 500 sick pilgrims with as many volunteers.

Part of the development at the Slipper Chapel during Fr. Connelly's time was a new open-sided church to replace the wooden structure erected by Fr. Scott James which was by now inadequate. The basic construction was completed and the new altar was in place by Easter 1973 and on Easter Monday Fr. Connelly offered the first Mass there with a small congregation. The altar, which is of polished Aberdeen granite, is the gift of the

Union of Catholic Mothers. Their pilgrimage is probably the largest annual pilgrimage. They always come on the first Tuesday in July and many travel overnight from long distances arriving in the early hours of the morning. In 1973 at their pilgrimage on 3rd July they were able to have the joy of assisting at the consecration by Bishop Grant of the altar which they had provided. By the end of that year, the number of pilgrims coming in organised parties had swollen to 36,223. One of the most notable of the events in 1973 had been the ecumenical pilgrimage when, for the first time, an Administrator of the Roman Catholic Shrine preached in the Anglican Shrine.

In August 1975 the long and very varied history of the Shrine was celebrated in drama, song and dance in the open air at the Slipper Chapel. The script of <u>Walsingham</u> was written by Terry Wynn, the music was arranged by Meg Toplis and the play was directed by Barbara Berkery who was responsible for the "Genesians", a Catholic-based group of actors. Later in the year it was repeated in Westminster Cathedral. The Genesians returned to Walsingham in 1976 and 1977.

There were more varied pilgrimages in 1976 with a Children's Day on 16th June and pilgrimages from the Co-workers of Mother Teresa and from Her Majesty's Armed Forces. In 1977 there was the first of a series of annual

Claude Fisher with Robert Runcie,
Archbishop of Canterbury, May 1980

Days of Prayer for Vocations held in May and also for the first time a Northern Men's Pilgrimage which left its mark by presenting the Pilgrim Club with a hundred pint mugs. Many dioceses of England now have their own annual pilgrimages and some of these have numbered thousands, the most notable of these being that of the Westminster Archdiocese in May

1980 when some 10,000 pilgrims accompanied Cardinal Hume and his five assistant Bishops. On this occasion Cardinal Hume went to the Anglican shrine to pray for Christian unity. When the Archbishop of Canterbury, Robert Runcie, led the Anglican National Pilgrimage with 15,000 people later in the same month, he reciprocated by going to the Slipper Chapel to light a candle and pray for the same unity for which Christ prayed.

The main pilgrimage each year is the Dowry of Mary Pilgrimage, which was originally called the National Pilgrimage which takes place on the Sunday nearest to Our Lady's birthday (which is also the anniversary of the consecration of the Slipper Chapel). Usually the Cardinal Archbishop of Westminster is the leader and every Cardinal since Cardinal Bourne has been a Walsingham pilgrim. In 1973, when Cardinal Heenan led the pilgrimage for the first time the police counted 6,500 for the procession. The Walsingham Newsletter for November 1973 comments, "All in all it was a great day and glorious sunshine enhanced the beauty of the open-air Mass and the colourful spectacle of the traditional procession along the Holy Mile."

In great contrast to this was the National Pilgrimage of the Holy Year, 1975. The Administrator of the Shrine at the time, Fr. Roland Connelly s.m. wrote this account:

"Preparations for the National Pilgrimage were made under a sweltering sun and no-one really accepted that it began to rain on the previous evening. We had grown too accustomed to the sun to believe that the National Pilgrimage could be washed out by rain. But it was.

"It rained all night and it rained all day. The first wet day in Walsingham for two months. The fords were impassable; the roads flooded; pilgrim coaches delayed; the parking field unusable. The Police worked magnificently with 23 officers on duty but they could not break the traffic blocks.

"The Mass started late with many people still on the way but the open-sided church emphasised its open-sidedness and the water poured in on the congregation and the concelebrants. Everything was wet including the

Pilgrims at Mass, National Pilgrimage, 1975

pilgrims. The Mass was abridged as much as possible at the express wish of Bishop Grant and the Pueri Cantores who had come all the way from London found little opportunity to demonstrate their talents. The water seeped into the public address system so that it could only work on half power and the gale roaring through the trees prevented most people from hearing anything at all ...

"The three thousand pilgrims who attended Mass were joined by another three thousand in the afternoon for the procession. The rain continued unabated and seemingly unheeded but the lanes were blocked by traffic and no coaches could move from the Slipper Chapel to the village. Many pilgrims waited at the Slipper Chapel for the procession to arrive; others, more hardy, made their way on foot through the water and then returned in solemn procession. Bishop Grant led the procession with all the Bishops, and then at the Slipper Chapel, Archbishop Carter of Kingston, Jamaica, gave Benediction of the Blessed Sacrament and Cardinal Heenan gave an abridged version of his address. And then with hundreds of cold damp pilgrims queuing for well-deserved cups of hot tea, the boilers broke down and even the comfort of a warming drink was denied them.

"The fool has said in his heart that this pilgrimage was a ghastly failure. Almost everything that could go wrong did go wrong and this is no reflection on the valiant body of volunteers and helpers who worked so assiduously. Fainthearts wonder if people will ever come again after such discouragement, but over-all the picture was not one of gloom and certainly there was no pessimism.

"On the contrary there was a most amazing spirit of happiness and acceptance. "The Lord gives, the Lord takes away. Blessed be the name of the Lord." The pilgrims accepted the weather as God's will and joyfully made the most of their circumstances. The young protected the old; umbrellas were shared by strangers; shelter and cosy nooks vacated by the strong in favour of the weak.

"This was not a pagan crowd bravely enduring its sufferings; it was a community of Christians aware of a challenge and determined to offer their sufferings to the Lord as a prayerful sacrifice of love.

"The local paper quoted an old lady saying, "This is the coldest wettest National Pilgrimage we have had in thirty years". I would say "This must be the best National Pilgrimage we have had in thirty years". (Walsingham Newsletter), November 1975).

In 1978, Walsingham lost two notable figures. In June, Fr. Connelly was moved and he was replaced temporarily by a pro-Administrator, Sister Kathleen Moran s.m., then superior of the community of the Marist Sisters, who work with the Fathers in Walsingham. On 3rd July, the day before "Mothers Day", Mr. Richard Pegg died. Dick, as he was known to all, had worked for the shrine in many capacities and was a familiar sight to thousands of pilgrims as he carried out his duties. "Zeal for my father's house has consumed me" was taken as a text for the homily at his funeral and changed to "Zeal for my Mother's house has consumed me" for the service of Our Lady of Walsingham was his vocation. He was given a shrine funeral on the 7th July when, robed in their shrine albs, the Volunteer Boys who had worked with him carried his coffin to the village churchyard. He was to be joined there two years later by his parish priest, Fr. John Murphy s.m., who had served the parish of Walsingham in the spirit of Mary for the previous 10 years.

In October a new Director of the Shrine was announced. He was Fr. Clive Birch s.m. who had been teaching in the Marist school in Sidcup. He celebrated his first Mass in the Slipper Chapel on 2nd November 1978 and took up his appointment in the following year. The tale of growth still continues and the shrine is going from strength to strength.

On 11th July, Feast of St. Benedict, 1980, Henry Martin Gillett became the first and only person to be interred in the Slipper Chapel. Born in 1902, he became the founder of the Ecumenical Society of the Blessed Virgin Mary. He did much to foster devotion to Our Lady and to restore the ancient shrines of England. He was made a Knight Commander of the Order of St. Gregory the Great and died on St. George's Day 1980.

History has a way of repeating itself and once again the open-air altar proved insufficient for the needs of the pilgrims. On 8th September 1980, the work of dismantling Fr. Connelly's altar was begun and shortly afterwards the building of a new pilgrim church was begun to be completed in

the late summer of 1981. It is a simple building in Saxon style constructed in brick and flint with a pantile roof in keeping with the rural buildings in the neighbourhood. The church can shelter about 700 pilgrims from the vagaries of the Norfolk climate and the wall behind the altar can be opened to allow the larger congregations which frequently gather to assist at Mass. At the National Pilgrimage on 6th September the almost completed church was blessed by Cardinal Hume. 1981 was also notable for the very first pilgrimage for the Deaf at Whitsun.

1982 was an "annus mirabilis" for the Shrine. At Easter a group of young people carried a huge wooden cross to the Slipper Chapel from Bletchley. It has been erected at the west door of the Chapel of Reconciliation and serves as a 15th Station of the Cross - the Resurrection. (It contains a relic of Padre Pio.) On 22nd May at the East Anglian Diocesan Pilgrimage Bishop Alan Clark solemnly consecrated the Chapel of Reconciliation and re-consecrated the granite altar which had been taken away during the building work, sealing into it the relics of St. Laurence, St. Thomas Becket and St Thomas More, which had been removed for safe-keeping, and adding to them a relic of the Marist martyr St. Peter Chanel. As the martyrs were entombed there was a pause and the sound of the banging of the trowel of a shrine workman - Tom Hair - filled the chapel. Tom was embarrassed and wanted to leave the finishing of the work till later but Bishop Alan urged him on: "It is good to hear it" he said.

Seven days later there was an even bigger event when Pope John Paul II visited Great Britain and celebrated Mass in Wembley Stadium. Faint hearts among the English Bishops had meant that a papal visit to the Shrine had been left out of the itinerary, but if Peter could not visit Mary, then she would go to see him and so it was that Walsingham came to Wembley.

Various suggestions had been made about getting the statue to London involving processions to the station at King's Lynn and from Liverpool Street, but in the event Our Lady of Walsingham was wrapped in a blanket and travelled in the boot of Fr. Birch's car to the Marist house at Kew Gardens. An unceremonious departure as in 1538 but at least this time the statue was going to be honoured and not burned.

The following morning at breakfast Fr. Birch announced that he had given Our Lady a bath and spruced up the paintwork. I went to look. He had done the painting by electric light and in the daylight the child's face appeared puce! "Clive," I said, "you can't leave it looking like that! He looks like he's having a stroke!" So, there and then, Clive repainted the statue and it went off to Wembley with the paint wet. (This wasn't the first time Fr. Birch had to repaint the statue. There was another occasion when one of the good sisters, who shall remain nameless, scrubbed the statue ready for Lent and literally wiped the smile from Our Lady's face!)

At Wembley the statue was lodged in the control room for safe-keeping because it had the precious crown on. Eventually we were taken to our dressing room where another problem surfaced. Because the statue had been in the bath the previous night the wood had swollen and it would no longer fit the sedilia. Having spent time in the control room I knew how to summon a carpenter and the sedilia was quickly altered.

Pope John Paul II venerates the Statue

Once in the arena, there was another set-back. Instead of being placed on the altar platform the pedestal for the statue was placed on the ground beside in an obscure position. Those of us in the escort party·were greatly disappointed in what we felt to be a lack of honour shown to Our Lady of Walsingham but we need not have worried. When the Holy Father came to preach he knew he was to refer to the presence of the statue of Our Lady of Walsingham but he could not see it so he sent his secretary to find it. Together with an M.C. he brought the statue in front of the Pope. At the end of his homily Pope John Paul beckoned for the statue and kissed the figures of Jesus and Mary. My heart was in my mouth, - "The paint is wet!" I thought. Fortunately the baking hot day had dried it out. Then the Pope did an astonishing thing. He ordered the statue to be placed on the altar for Mass despite the protestations of the rubrically-correct M.C. The Magnificat came to mind: "He has raised up the lowly" Our Lady of Walsingham was raised from obscurity and publicly venerated by the Vicar of Christ. "Son, behold your mother."

At the end of the Mass, after the Pope had departed, we defied the instructions we had been given and carried the statue on a lap of honour round the stadium with the vast crowds breaking into hymns of Our Lady as the statue came near. Appropriately, Our Lady left by the Royal Tunnel!

Back in Walsingham, the statue was first taken to visit the Anglican shrine and was placed on the altar of the Holy House as a symbol of prayer for the unity of Christians before being carried down the Holy Mile to the Slipper Chapel. There was another significant ecumenical moment at the Feast of the Assumption when a joint Catholic-Anglican Sunday service was televised from the Chapel of Reconciliation.

1982 was also the year of a great grace when the Carmel of Our Lady of Walsingham was established in nearby Langham. It had not been possible to find a suitable property in the village itself for the Carmel but nevertheless it forms an integral part of the Shrine with the sisters forming a powerhouse of prayer and contemplation to sustain the work of the Shrine. In a truly Marian way, it is a hidden and almost unknown work which bears great fruit.

To mark their 70th anniversary in 1983 the U.C.M. commissioned a new processional statue by the local artist Jane Quail. Carved in oak it proved too heavy for the mothers to carry and had to be hollowed out. When not in use it is housed in the Carmel chapel.

Also in 1983 there was a reorganization of the Pilgrim Bureau. Formerly there had been pilgrim hostels in Aelred House, Dow House, Falcon House, Guisborough House and Elmham House. With the building of a new wing at Elmham House all the beds could be gathered together. At the same time the administration was consolidated in the old school in Friday Market.

The Golden Jubilee of the 1934 translation of the Shrine from King's Lynn to the Slipper Chapel was kept in 1984, but the year was marked by a sad event. On 16th March Fr. Bruno Scott James, the first Priest-Custodian, who looked after the Shrine from 1935-1944 died. In his autobiography, "Asking for Trouble" he describes his conversion:

"One day, driven to the verge of desperation by the awful choice that seemed to lie ahead of me, I walked out to the Slipper Chapel and, having obtained the key from the custodian, threw myself on my knees and implored God to give me the grace to follow his will whatever the cost might be and wherever it might lead me. I then vowed, hardly realising what I said, that if Our Lady would obtain from her Son this grace for me I would devote my life to her service at Walsingham …. Three months later - three of the most painful and agonising months I have ever known - I was received into the Catholic Church."

An ecumenical event of a different kind occurred on 8th July. The icon of the Mother of God of Walsingham was dedicated and enthroned. The icon had been written by the priest in charge of St. Seraphim's Orthodox Church

 in Walsingham, Archimandrite David. The ceremonies began at St. Seraphim's and then the procession made its way to the Slipper Chapel. The icon was preceded by three deacons with censers, Brother John and Brother Peter from the Shrine and Brother Elias from the Orthodox church together with Fr. Birch and Archimandrite David. As the Lourdes hymn was sung and we reached the words "We pray for his Vicar, our Father and Rome" Fr. Birch turned to the Archimandrite and said "You

will have to excuse this verse, Father!" It was a blisteringly hot day and there was a fear that the icon would be damaged so Tomas McVeigh the Guestmaster was given the gruelling task of shielding the icon with an ombrellino all the way down the Holy Mile. At the Slipper Chapel the Akathist was sung and the icon enthroned.

For the Feast of the Assumption and the anniversary of the jubilee a magnificent festival of flowers and music was arranged by the Shrine deacon, Brother John Hawkes. At the end of the celebrations the Guild of Our Lady of Ransom carried the statue from the King's Lynn Holy House to Walsingham and then presented a replica of it to the Church of the Annunciation in Friday Market.

A new Shrine Director was appointed in 1985 when Fr. Peter Allen s.m. came to replace Fr. Birch. In this year, also, Walsingham said adieu to Claude Fisher who died on 14th May. Let Fr. Bruno Scott James speak again: "Here I must pay a tribute to my pilgrimage secretary, Mr Claude Fisher. He was with me and co-operating with me from the very first. I could not have even begun the work without his help. Not even my greatest friends have ever thought I was an easy person to work with, yet Claude Fisher never faltered. He gave himself generously and without thought of himself. He did the work and took the kicks while I got the credit. Did two pilgrimages arrive at the same time both claiming precedence, Claude Fisher was there to straighten things out; did five thousand pilgrims arrive without warning and demand food, if not lodging, Claude Fisher was there to arrange everything. The revival of Walsingham was due largely to his selfless and unobtrusive devotion " (Bruno Scott James "Asking for Trouble").

In 1986 the Blessed Sacrament was re-positioned in the Chapel of Reconciliation in a silver tabernacle originally made in 1948 for a convent chapel in Edinburgh.

1987 was declared by the Pope to be a Marian Year and the beginning of what he saw as an "advent" leading up to the Millennium. At the Shrine, which was one of the designated holy places for gaining the Holy Year indulgence, development continued. Work began on refurbishing and extending the service area built in 1971. It re-emerged as a new cloister in sympathy with the Chapel of Reconciliation. The statue and Slipper Chapel reredos were repainted and gilded by Siegfried Pietsch and to keep them in pristine condition the contro-versial decision was taken by the Shrine Council to exclude votive candles from the Chapel. These now burn in a new Holy Ghost Chapel formed from the former sacristy which in turn moved into the old chapel. The Marian Year was closed at the Assumption in 1988 when the Papal Nuncio, Archbishop Luigi Barbarito, presided at Mass and re-crowned the statue as his predecessor had done in the previous Marian Year of 1954. 1988 also saw a recording of the BBC programme "Songs of Praise"in the Priory grounds on 16th July.

With the increase in number and size of the diocesan pilgrimages the National Pilgrimage in September had waned and so in 1989 it was decided to re-launch it as the Dowry of Mary Pilgrimage and the Cardinal Archbishop of Westmin-ster continued to be the principal pilgrim.

Blessing of the Font, Holy Saturday 1996

The provision of holy water had long been a problem at the Shrine since pilgrims had a demand which often exceeded supply. This was remedied by the provision of a permanent holy water font in the new cloister. The font itself is 14th century and is from the redundant church of St. Mary at Forncett St. Mary near Norwich. It stands in a flint basin, the work of one of the last flintknappers of Suffolk, John Lord of Brandon. Set in the flint are stone panels depicting water as a symbol of God's grace. They are by Jane Quail.

The patronal feast of the Shrine - the Annunciation - 1990 was marked in a sad way by the theft of the crown from Our Lady's head. Fortunately - if it can be put that way - it was the "daily" crown and not the precious one which is only used on great Feasts. The local deanery came to the rescue and paid for a replacement which was placed on the statue on 6th April 1991 by Bishop Alan Clark in a gesture of reparation for the sacrilege.

Joyful, sorrowful and glorious events mix frequently in Walsingham reflecting the mystery of the Incarnation. In 1991 we said farewell to another faithful servant of Walsingham, Miss Bernadette Doyle. She was sacristan of the Church of the Annunciation in Friday Market where, like Anna in St Luke's Gospel, "she never left the temple, serving God night and day" in a truly Marian unobtrusive way. In May three members of staff were ordained: Russell Frost to the priesthood and Paul Hirons and Bernard Warwick to the diaconate. August saw the first "Walsingham Variations" festival organised by the Director of Music, Nigel Kerry, who wanted, as he said, "a festival celebrating the Arts whose very existence derives from the reckless creativity of God revealed in the Word made Flesh." September 1991 was a milestone for the Guild of Our Lady of Ransom whose men made their 40th walk from London to Walsingham.

Another sacrilege was made on 4th July 1992 when the statue was attacked. The back of the throne and fingers and thumb of the figures were broken. After being expertly restored by Mr. John Howse of Walsingham and Brother Leon from the Orthodox community, the statue was reinstalled on 6th September. July 1992 also saw the presentation of a fine illuminated manuscript containing meditations on the Stations of the Cross and recollections of the great cross-carrying pilgrimage of 1948. The priest who was responsible for Walsingham in 1948, Fr. Gerry Langley - a much-loved and holy man - died on Christmas Eve 1992. He, too, was a great lover of Walsingham.

A new year in 1993 found a new Director of the Shrine in Fr. Alan Williams s.m. who replaced Fr. Peter Allen. Fr. Williams arrived just in time to find Elmham House flooded by a burst pipe which had brought several ceilings down - a true initiation into the practicalities of looking after the Shrine. At Easter, the Sunday Mass celebrated by Bishop Alan Clark was televised allowing many throughout the country to share in the Shrine's worship. On 9th October the Walsingham Association celebrated its Diamond Jubilee with a Mass in Westminster Cathedral.

On 5th July 1994, Lilian Dagless died. Together with her brother James she was responsible for carving the reredos in the Slipper Chapel and the pedestal and canopy of the Shrine.

Anniversaries continued in 1995 when on the 17th May a group of American servicemen and their families from RAF Lakenheath came with their chaplain to celebrate Mass in the Priory crypt in commemoration of the 50th anniversary of the first Mass in the Priory since the reformation. This had been organised by the American forces in East Anglia in 1945. The Union of Catholic Mothers also celebrated their Golden Jubilee pilgrimage on 3rd July. Meanwhile on 11th June, Bishop Peter Smith led his first pilgrimage as Bishop of East Anglia.

Jubilees point to the development of the Shrine and its establishment in the life of the church in England but there is also a growth in the development of the Shrine's influence in the wider world. 1996 was a good example of this with visits from a rosary group from Atlanta, Georgia, USA: the Caribbean pilgrimage: the Tamil pilgrimage: Archbishop Adrian Smith s.m. from Honiara in the Solomon Islands: Archbishop John Quinn from San Francisco and Fr. Luciano Guerra, the Rector of Fatima.

The 1997 pilgrimage season was the usual rich tapestry of the Catholic Church but the highlight was of course the beginning of the Centenary Year commemorating the restoration of the Shrine of Our Lady of Walsingham at King's Lynn in 1897 and the first pilgrimage of modern times. Tuesday 19th August was the 100th anniversary of the King's Lynn shrine and so celebrations were focussed there. Much preparation had been made in advance and an early start was made on the day when at 8.30a.m. a coach load of staff and volunteers set off for Lynn to make the final arrangements. Three tents (reminiscent of Mount Tabor!) had been set up in The Walks in the shadow of the medieval chapel of Our Lady of the Mount where pilgrims had once rested and prayed.

Meanwhile the Guild of Our Lady of Ransom was recreating the 1897 arrival of Pope Leo XIII's statue from London. Our Lady arrived (as she did 100 years ago) on the 10.19 from Liverpool Street to be greeted like a celebrity by the waiting press and cameramen. The Ransomers then carried the statue to the Catholic Church where it was re-enshrined in the newly refurbished Holy House. The Friday Market replica statue was then brought in procession to the Red Mount. There, on a roasting hot day under a cloudless Norfolk blue sky Pontifical Mass was sung by the Bishop of East Anglia in the presence of Cardinal Cahal Daly and a large congregation including the Mayor of Kings Lynn with an impressive civic party including no less than four mace bearers, a sword bearer and a staff bearer! After Mass the Ransomers carried the statue to Walsingham halting at Massingham and Fakenham where the statue was lodged in the church overnight.

The following day dawned as another sweltering day in what the weathermen assured us was the hottest August ever - very different from the rainy day of the first pilgrimage in 1897. The Shrine staff began the day with an eager scanning of the dailies for coverage of yesterday's events then it was down to business. At the Slipper Chapel all was a hive of activity as choir and musicians rehearsed, servers were put through their paces, stewards made their arrangements and last minute details were attended to in the sacristy. Then, just after 11 o'clock, the Slipper Chapel bell rang out to announce the arrival of the statue of Our Lady carried by the Ransomers this morning from Fakenham. It was received by Cardinal Daly, Bishop Smith and Bishop Clark.

*Mgr. Stark, Master of the Guild of Our Lady of Ransom
and the Ransom Walkers near the Slipper Chapel*

Then at 12 noon, after the recitation of the Angelus the Centenary Mass began under a glorious blue sky. The Mass lasted over an hour and a half with music specially composed for the occasion. Over 70 priests concelebrated with the three bishops and about 2,000 people. A far cry from the 40 pilgrims who came in the rain in 1897 to pray outside an unused Slipper Chapel. After Mass, during which the Cardinal preached an inspiring sermon on the history and spirituality of Walsingham and its relevance to the present as we stand on the threshold of the third millennium, the clergy went in procession to the Slipper Chapel where the Cardinal unveiled and dedicated the striking West window depicting the Annunciation. It is the work of Alfred Fisher and the gift of the Guild of Our Lady of Ransom.

After a brief break for lunch the procession formed to make its way to the village. For the first time the College of Guardians of the Anglican Shrine (several of whom are now Catholics) walked the Holy Mile in a gesture of unity. As members of the Guild of Chaplains of the Shrine led the recitation of the fifteen mysteries of the rosary the Royal Air Force added its own contribution with the familiar (to East Anglians) roar of Tornado fighters reminding the pilgrims of the constant need for prayer for peace and reconciliation ..

"Lady of Walsingham, Lady of England,
lead us on in the work for peace.
May love and justice guide all the nations,
war and strife for ever cease ......"

On arrival at the Priory site Bishop Smith gave Benediction of the Blessed Sacrament and then a visit was made to the site of the Holy House where the statue had been placed. The Bishop began the devotions by leading the Eternal Rest for the repose of the soul of Mrs. Ann Gurney, wife of the owner of the priory, who had died that morning. Then, accompanied by the Ransomers and members of the Walsingham parish, the statue was returned to Friday Market church where it remains, as Fr. Peter Allen, the parish priest, said "as a reminder of all that has happened in the past 100 years and of the debt of gratitude Walsingham owes to the Guild of Ransom." In true pilgrimage style the evening was given up to a great party in the field beside the Slipper Chapel culminating in a triumphant firework display.

The following day the Shrine was back to normal. The 12 noon Pilgrim Mass was celebrated with groups from Shropshire and Birmingham; a party made the Stations of the Cross, there was the usual Rosary in the Slipper Chapel at 2.30pm and in the Chapel of Reconciliation, Adoration of the Blessed Sacrament at 3pm with Vespers and Benediction at 4pm. So began the next 100 years.

At the present time, Walsingham is beginning to re-emerge as the National Shrine of England in fact as well as in name and what St. Jerome unsuspectingly said is proving true: "et de Hierusolymis et de Britannia aequaliter potet aula coelestis." - the court of Heaven can be reached as well from Britain as from Jerusalem.

SOURCES CONSULTED

Bond, H. A.	The Walsingham story through 900 Years Walsingham: Guild Shop, Revised 1988
Bond, H. A. and Fisher, C.	The Story of Walsingham Walsingham: Greenhoe Press, 1950
Connelly, Rev. R. W.	Walsingham Information for School Projects Walsingham: Pilgrim Bureau (1971)
	The Slipper Chapel Great Wakering: Mayhew-McCrimmon, 1975
	Walsingham is for Today London: Catholic Truth Society, 1972
	Walsingham Pilgrim Book: a guide to the Shrine Great Wakering: Mayhew-McCrimmon, 1975
	"Our Lady of Walsingham" article in Acta Societatis Mariae, December 1968
Dickinson, Rev. J. C.	The Shrine of Our Lady of Walsingham Cambridge: Cambridge University Press, 1956
	Monastic Life in Medieval England London: Black, 1961
Fisher, C.	Walsingham Lives on London: Catholic Truth Society, 1979
Fletcher, Rev. P.	Recollections of a Ransomer London: Sands & Co, 1928
Gilbert, Rev.	What to see in Walsingham: an historical guide book Walsingham: Greyfriars, 1939

Graystone, Rev. G.   Our Lord's House at Nazareth
                          London: Catholic Truth Society, 1963

Gillett, H. M.   Famous Shrines of Our Lady
                          London: Samuel Walker, (2 vols), 1961

Mortimer, Rev. C. G.   Our Lady of Walsingham
                          London: Catholic Truth Society, 1956

Oldmeadow, Ernest   Francis Cardinal Bourne
                          London: Burns, Oates & Washbourne, 1944

Rollings, Rev. P.   Walsingham in Times Past
                          Brinscall: Countryside Publications, 1981

Sandell, Rev. W.   "Our Lady of Walsingham" article in
                          The Clergy Review, vol XI, no.6, June 1936

Scott James, Bruno   Asking for trouble
                          London: Darton, Longman & Todd, 1962

Ward, Rev. A.   Walsingham and the Annunciation of the Lord
                          Unpublished Thesis

Waterton, Edmund   Pietas Mariana Britannica
                          London: St. Joseph's Catholic Library, 1879

Whatmore, Rev. L. E.   Highway to Walsingham
                          Walsingham: Pilgrim Bureau, 1973

Yaxley, David   A Portrait of Norfolk
                          London: Roberts, 1977